LeBron James
King of the Court

by Tom Sibila

Reading Consultant:
Timothy Rasinski, Ph.D.
Professor of Reading Education
Kent State University

Content Consultant:
David Lee Morgan, Jr.
Sports Writer
The Akron Beacon Journal

Red Brick™ Learning

Published by Red Brick™ Learning
7825 Telegraph Road, Bloomington, Minnesota 55438
http://www.redbricklearning.com

Library of Congress Cataloging-in-Publication Data
Sibila, Tom.
    LeBron James: king of the court / by Tom Sibila; reading
consultant, Timothy Rasinski.
        p. cm.—(High five reading)
        Includes bibliographical references and index.
        ISBN 13: 978-0-7368-5737-6 (hard cover)
        ISBN 10: 0-7368-5737-0 (hard cover)
        ISBN 13: 978-0-7368-5747-5 (soft cover)
        ISBN 10: 0-7368-5747-8 (soft cover)
        1. James, LeBron—Juvenile literature. 2. Basketball players—
United States—Biography—Juvenile literature.
I. Rasinski, Timothy V. II. Title. III. Series.
GV884.J36S53 2006
796.323'092—dc22
                                2005010402

Created by Kent Publishing Services, Inc.
Designed by Signature Design Group, Inc.
Edited by Jerry Ruff, Managing Editor, Red Brick™ Learning
Red Brick™ Learning Editorial Director: Mary Lindeen

Photo Credits: Cover, pages 8, 18, Patty Burdon; pages 4, 6, 22, 31, 34, 36,
Phil Masturzo; page 10, Lucy Nicholson, Agence France Presse; page 12, Phil
Masturzo, Akron Beacon Journal/Associated Press; page 17, Ed Suba, Jr., KRT
Photos; page 21, Karen Schiley, Akron Beacon Journal/Associated Press; page
26, Jay LaPrete, Associated Press; page 28, Corbis; page 32, Michael Lilly,
Associated Press; pages 38, 40, Icon Sports Media/SMI

Printed in the United States of America.

2 3 4 5 6 11 10 09 08 07 06

Table of Contents

*TV announcer Dick Vitale meets with
LeBron James before the game.*

*LeBron warms up in front
of an ESPN 2 TV crew.*

CHAPTER 1

Fame

The gym was packed. Almost 2 million people were watching on TV. All this fuss was for a high school basketball game. Why? LeBron James was playing!

Putting on a Show

On December 12, 2002, LeBron James was pumped. "I can't wait for the game," he said. "I'm going to put on a show."

LeBron did just that. He scored 31 points. He grabbed 13 **rebounds**. His team, Saint Vincent-Saint Mary, beat Oak Hill Academy 65–45. Oak Hill was the top high school team in the United States.

The TV announcer yelled, "(LeBron) is the truth, the whole truth, and nothing but the truth!"

rebound (REE-bound): a ball that someone grabs after a shot

LeBron poses with the cover of Sports Illustrated.

The Chosen One

LeBron was a high school superstar. **Professional** athletes came to his games. **NFL** star Jerome Bettis came to watch LeBron. So did **NBA** all-star Allen Iverson.

Other famous people wanted to see LeBron, too. Rapper Beanie Sigel came to one game. Rapper Freeway was there, too. Jay-Z came, but the game was sold out!

LeBron was called the greatest high school basketball player ever. *Sports Illustrated* magazine put him on the cover. They called LeBron "The Chosen One."

---

professional (pruh-FESH-uh-nuhl): making money for something others do for fun
NFL: short for *National Football League*
NBA: short for *National Basketball Association*

Hickory Street in Akron, Ohio, where LeBron James grew up

A Hard Start

LeBron did not start out famous. No one knew this kid from the **ghetto** would one day play in the NBA.

As a child, LeBron had a hard family life. He lived in **public housing**. He didn't always do well at school.

So how do you think LeBron made it? Was it just his talent? Did he do it all on his own? What do you think?

ghetto (GE-toh): a part of a city or town where poor people live

public housing (PUHB-lik HOU-zing): houses or apartments that the government builds for people who have little money

LeBron's mother, Gloria James, has always been his number-one fan.

Chapter 2

Family

LeBron James was born poor. His mother was 16 and in high school. LeBron didn't know his father. Life was hard. But there was love.

Raised by Mom

LeBron James was born on December 30, 1984, in Akron, Ohio. He was raised by his mother, Gloria. Life was a struggle. The two moved from place to place.

But Gloria loved LeBron. She tried her best to raise him. She tried to protect him from the drugs and **violence** in the ghetto. It was not easy.

---

violence (VYE-uh-luhnss): force used to injure someone or cause damage

Eddie Jackson was like a father to LeBron.

First Home

LeBron and Gloria lived with Gloria's mother, Freda James. Gloria's boyfriend lived with them, too. His name was Eddie Jackson. Eddie also was poor.

Freda cared deeply about people. Eddie once said, "To meet Gloria's mother, you would've met the most wonderful person in the world."

At Freda's house, LeBron had a real family life. He loved his mother and grandmother. Eddie liked LeBron. LeBron thought of Eddie as his father.

First Hoops

It was Christmas Eve. LeBron was almost
4 years old. Gloria and Eddie had bought a
toy basketball set for him.

Early in the morning, Eddie heard a thump.
He ran into the kitchen. There he found
Freda on the floor. She had died of a heart
attack. Freda was only 42 years old.

Gloria did not tell LeBron right away.
It was Christmas. She wanted him to enjoy
his present. Gloria watched as LeBron ran
to the hoop and slam-dunked the ball.
Eddie kept moving the hoop higher.
As Eddie watched, he said, "Man, this kid
has some **elevation** for just being 3 years old!"

---

elevation (el-uh-VAY-shuhn): the ability to jump high

From Bad to Worse

Freda's death was hard on the family.
Gloria and Eddie did not take care of Freda's
house. It started to fall apart. They had to
move out. Eddie went to live with his aunt.
Gloria and LeBron were alone.

Gloria moved to the **projects**. There were
drug dealers, gangs, and shootings there.
Gloria did her best to protect LeBron.
But she was getting into trouble herself.
It began to affect her son. In fourth grade,
LeBron missed 87 days of school.

projects (PRAH-jekts): a group of houses or apartments
built for poor people to live in

New Beginning

LeBron had problems. Luckily, his Pee Wee football coach noticed. The coach's name was Frankie Walker. Frankie also knew LeBron's mother was having a hard time. He talked with Gloria. They agreed that LeBron could live with Frankie's family.

"It was a new beginning for me," LeBron said later. He didn't miss a single day of school in fifth grade. The Walkers showed him **discipline**, too. "That was a huge step," LeBron said.

Other people also helped LeBron as a boy. Who do you think they were?

---

discipline (DISS-uh-plin): control over the way you or other people behave

Caring adults helped LeBron as a boy. Today, LeBron is able to help children by teaching them to read and urging them to work hard in school.

LeBron, standing in the back row next to his coach with his AAU team

CHAPTER 3

Friends

Imagine you are on a very good basketball team. Your teammates are your best friends. Then a new player joins the team. He is selfish. You don't like him. How can you win with a player like this?

The Shooting Stars

In fifth grade, LeBron played on a **local** basketball team. The team was called the Shooting Stars. Also on the team were Dru Joyce, Jr., Sian Cotton, and Willie McGee. The four became close friends. They called themselves the Fab Four.

---

local (LOH-kuhl): near your house, or to do with the area where you live

National Champs

The Shooting Stars were good. So good, they made it to a **national tournament**. This contest was held in Salt Lake City, Utah. It was the first time any of the boys had been on a plane. LeBron cried for much of the flight.

LeBron felt better later, though. In fact, he played so well he was named the **MVP** of the tournament. His team won first place for their age group.

The Fab Four stuck together. They won more than 200 games. They also won six national **titles**. But all that was only the beginning.

---

national tournament (NASH-uh-nuhl TUR-nuh-muhnt): a contest in which teams from the same country compete
MVP: short for *Most Valuable Player*
title (TYE-tuhl): a championship

Dru Joyce, Jr., the shortest member of the Fab Four, went on to play basketball in college.

High School

In eighth grade, the Fab Four made a **pact**. They promised to play at the same high school together. They also promised to win a state title. The boys chose to go to Saint Vincent-Saint Mary. In their first year, they kept their promise. They won the state title.

---

pact (PAKT): an agreement among a group of people

The 6-foot-4 inch LeBron scored 25 points in the title game. But the big hero was "Little" Dru. The 5-foot-6-inch point guard shot seven three-pointers—and made all seven! At the end of the game, LeBron and his teammates lifted Dru into the air. The fans cheered, "Druuuuuuu!"

Sian Cotton, LeBron James, Dru Joyce, Jr., Romeo Travis, and Willie McGee

A New Face

The Fab Four had been playing together for six years. They had built a strong friendship. On and off the court, they **respected** each other. They shared. They acted like brothers. Then a new member joined the team.

Romeo Travis came to Saint Vincent-Saint Mary from another school. Romeo was a good player. But he was rough and selfish. Romeo did not get along with the Fab Four.

Sian later said, "I didn't like Romeo at all. He was selfish. He didn't know how to share. I'm talking about sharing your friendship and your feelings, and you know, love for a **brotha'**. We shared everything."

---

respect (ri-SPEKT): to admire or to think highly of someone
brotha' (BRUHTH-uh): a close friend

"Get What You Can Get"

Romeo didn't like the Fab Four, either. "I didn't like Sian," he said later. "I hated Dru. I hated to give up anything. I was so selfish that I would eat my food, and if I was full, I wouldn't ask anybody if they wanted some. I [had] learned that you had to get what you could get."

The Fab Four knew that their success came from sharing and trusting each other. Romeo didn't seem to get it.

Learning a Lesson

LeBron and his friends decided to teach Romeo a lesson. They would treat Romeo like he treated them. Maybe then Romeo would learn that to get along on their team, he had to share.

One day, Romeo was eating candy. A teammate had bought doughnuts. Romeo really wanted one. But no one was sharing with him. Then one of the boys asked Romeo for candy. Here was his chance. Romeo gave the boy some.

Willie McGee (left) and Romeo Travis smile and hug after winning the Ohio 2003 Division II State Championship.

For the first time, Romeo had shared something with his teammates. He had begun to learn to give and not just take. That day, the Fab Four became the Fab Five!

The Fab Five won two more state titles. In 2003, they were the top high school team in the United States.

More Problems Ahead

LeBron learned early that being a winner wasn't about being a star. Respect for his teammates mattered more. To win, they had to work together. To work together, they had to share. To share, they had to be unselfish.

But LeBron was also a star. Being a star brought many **challenges**. What do you think they were?

---

challenge (CHAL-uhnj): something difficult that takes extra work or effort

LeBron dunks the ball for a photographer.

CHAPTER 4

Pressure

Imagine you are 18 years old. Any place you go,
*people know you. They want your **autograph**.*
Big companies want you to sell things for them.
On the basketball court, people expect you to play
*great in every game. Each day, the **pressure** gets worse.*

Locked Doors

Already in high school, LeBron was famous.
More and more reporters came to his games.
People sneaked into the gym to watch him.
The school had to lock its doors at practice
to keep people away from LeBron. All this
attention started to **affect** LeBron.

---

autograph (AW-tuh-graf): a person's handwritten signature
pressure (PRE-shur): a burden or strain
affect (uh-FEKT): to change someone or something

Autographs

LeBron was on the cover of *Sports Illustrated*. Hundreds of people asked him to sign their copy of the magazine. At first, he was happy to do this—especially for kids. But then it became a problem.

Adults began to send their kids to get LeBron's autograph. Then the adults would sell the autographs! LeBron became angry. He said, "Everybody comes up to me, all these grown folks, asking for autographs, talking about it for their kids. Next thing you know, they're selling it on **eBay**."

Finally, LeBron got fed up. He quit signing the magazine covers.

---

eBay (EE-bay): a company that helps people sell things through the Internet

The Hummer

On LeBron's 18th birthday, his mother gave him a present. It was a new Hummer **SUV**. Gloria added a DVD player, three TVs, and a video game player. She ordered leather seats with "King James" printed on them. With all this, the SUV cost about $80,000.

Gloria had no job. She collected **welfare**. She lived in low-rent housing. People asked how she could pay for such a costly gift.

LeBron's new Hummer

SUV: short for *sport utility vehicle*
welfare (WEL-fair): money or other help given by a government to people who are in need

Watching LeBron

The Ohio High School Athletic Association (OHSAA) makes rules for high school athletes in Ohio. One rule is that athletes cannot use their **fame** to get money or gifts. If the athletes break the rule, they can't play. The OHSAA wanted to know about LeBron's Hummer. They wanted to know where the money to buy it came from.

But Gloria would not tell where she got the money. This made it worse for LeBron. The OHSAA began to watch him carefully.

LeBron plays with a toy Hummer before a game.

---

fame (FAYM): being well-known

More Trouble

One day, LeBron and his friends were at a store. LeBron knew the store's owner. He was a friend of Eddie Jackson's. The owner gave LeBron two **throwback jerseys**. LeBron said, "You don't have to do that, but thank you." He accepted the jerseys. They were worth $845.

To accept the jerseys broke the OHSAA rules. The OHSAA **suspended** LeBron for two games. Gloria was angry. She hired a lawyer to help them. Now people wondered where she got the money to pay the lawyer.

---

throwback jersey (THROH-bak JUR-zee): a basketball shirt that players wore in an earlier time
suspend (suh-SPEND): to punish by not letting a person take part in something

The fans loved LeBron's dunks.

Moving On

LeBron had a lot of problems. Still, his basketball coach stood up for him. He said LeBron had handled his problems well for someone so young.

LeBron blamed only himself for his problems. "I've been through **adversity** my whole life," he said. "Blaming other people is the easy way out. I blame myself. I'm glad it was me because it made me a better person. It made me stronger."

---

adversity (ad-VUR-suh-tee): when things are not easy

*NBA Commissioner David Stern shakes hands
with LeBron at the 2003 NBA draft.*

CHAPTER 5

Success

*The date was June 26, 2003. The NBA was holding its **draft**. NBA **Commissioner** David Stern announced, "With the first pick in the 2003 NBA draft, the Cleveland Cavaliers pick LeBron James."*

Staying Home

LeBron's dream had come true! He was an NBA player. Also, he could play near his hometown. Cleveland was only a 30-minute drive from where he grew up. Now his mom and friends could come to his games. He was still only 18 years old.

---

draft (DRAFT): a meeting where teams pick players for their team
commissioner (kuh-MISH-uh-nur): the person in charge of a professional sport

LeBron James during his rookie year in the NBA

Rookie Year

LeBron was also under pressure once again. Was he good enough to play in the NBA? Was he too young? Should he have gone to college first? Would he be an NBA star? Or would he be an NBA **bust**?

LeBron answered those questions in his first NBA game. He made the first shot he took. He went on to score 25 points. He had nine **assists**, six rebounds, and four steals.

LeBron led the Cavaliers out of last place. In fact, they almost made the **play-offs**. LeBron was named **Rookie** of the Year. In 2006, the Cavaliers did make the play-offs. LeBron also was named to the All-NBA First Team.

bust (BUHST): a failure
assist (uh-SIST): a pass to a player who then scores
play-off (PLAY-awf): a series of contests to decide a champion
rookie (RUH-kee): a player in his or her first year

King James slams another dunk.

To the Top?

LeBron started life with many **obstacles**. But he also had many gifts. He had a mother who loved him. He had adults who coached and cared about him. He had close friends to share with. He had basketball to enjoy.

With these gifts, LeBron became a success. He also learned he needed other people. He learned that a superstar can only win with a team. He learned to be **loyal** and unselfish. This was the way to true success.

LeBron's NBA career is just beginning. But one thing is certain: He is the truth, the whole truth, and nothing but the truth!

obstacle (OB-stuh-kuhl): something that makes it hard for you to do something
loyal (LOI-uhl): firm in giving support; faithful

Epilogue

LeBron James Highlights

Became first **sophomore** to be named Ohio Mr. Basketball in 2001. Won this title three years in a row.

First sophomore to be named to the *USA Today* All-USA 1st Team in 2001

Named High School Basketball Player of the Year by *USA Today* in 2002, 2003

Holds Saint Vincent-Saint Mary record for most points scored in one game with 52

Had 2,657 points, 892 rebounds, and 523 assists in high school

Named First Team all-state in football as a wide receiver

---

sophomore (SAHF-mor): a person in the second year of high school or college

Picked for McDonald's All-American Game in 2003 and named MVP of that game

Named *Parade Magazine* High School Basketball Player of the Year in 2002, 2003

Member of the 2004 U.S. Olympic men's basketball team

Youngest player ever to win NBA Rookie of the Year award

Averaged 20.9 points in his NBA rookie season—13th best in the league

Became youngest player ever to score 40 or more points in an NBA game

Became youngest player ever to have a **triple-double** in the NBA

triple-double (TRIP-uhl-DUH-buhl): to get double figures (10 or more) in three areas in one basketball game; the areas are points scored, rebounds, steals, or assists

Glossary

adversity (ad-VUR-suh-tee): when things are not easy

affect (uh-FEKT): to change someone or something

assist (uh-SIST): a pass to a player who then scores

autograph (AW-tuh-graf): a person's handwritten signature

brotha' (BRUHTH-uh): a close friend

bust (BUHST): a failure

challenge (CHAL-uhnj): something difficult that takes extra work or effort

commissioner (kuh-MISH-uh-nur): the person in charge of a professional sport

discipline (DISS-uh-plin): control over the way you or other people behave

draft (DRAFT): a meeting where teams pick players for their team

eBay (EE-bay): a company that helps people sell things through the Internet

elevation (el-uh-VAY-shuhn): the ability to jump high

fame (FAYM): being well-known

ghetto (GE-toh): a part of a city or town where poor people live

local (LOH-kuhl): near your house, or to do with the area where you live

loyal (LOI-uhl): firm in giving support; faithful

MVP: short for *Most Valuable Player*

national tournament (NASH-uh-nuhl TUR-nuh-muhnt): a contest in which teams from the same country compete

NBA: short for *National Basketball Association*

NFL: short for *National Football League*

obstacle (OB-stuh-kuhl): something that makes it hard for you to do something

pact (PAKT): an agreement among a group of people

play-off (PLAY-awf): a series of contests to decide a champion

pressure (PRE-shur): a burden or strain

professional: (pruh-FESH-uh-nuhl): making money for something others do for fun

projects (PRAH-jekts): a group of houses or apartments built for poor people to live in

public housing (PUHB-lik HOU-zing): houses or apartments that the government builds for people who have little money

rebound (REE-bound): a ball that someone grabs after a shot

respect (ri-SPEKT): to admire or to think highly of someone

rookie (RUH-kee): a player in his or her first year

sophomore (SAHF-mor): a person in the second year of high school or college

suspend (suh-SPEND): to punish by not letting a person take part in something

SUV: short for *sport utility vehicle*

throwback jersey (THROH-bak JUR-zee): a basketball shirt that players wore in an earlier time

title (TYE-tuhl): a championship

triple-double (TRIP-uhl-DUH-buhl): to get double figures (10 or more) in three areas in one basketball game; the areas are points scored, rebounds, steals, or assists

violence (VYE-uh-luhnss): force used to injure someone or cause damage

welfare (WEL-fair): money or other help given by a government to people who are in need

Bibliography

Butler, Robbie. *The Harlem Globetrotters: Clown Princes of Basketball.* High Five Reading. Bloomington, Minn.: Red Brick Learning, 2002.

Houghton, Sarah. *Michael Jordan: The Best Ever.* High Five Reading. Bloomington, Minn.: Red Brick Learning, 2002.

Mattern, Joanne. *LeBron James: Young Basketball Star.* Robbie Readers. Hockessin, Del.: Mitchell Lane Publishers, 2005.

Morgan, David Lee, Jr. *LeBron James: The Rise of a Star.* Cleveland: Gray & Company Publishers, 2003.

Savage, Jeff. *LeBron James.* Amazing Athletes. Minneapolis: Lerner Publishing Group, 2005.

Useful Addresses

Cleveland Cavaliers
One Center Court
Cleveland, OH 44115

LeBronJames.com
1507 W. Market St
Akron, OH 44313

National Basketball Association
645 Fifth Avenue
New York, NY 10022

Internet Sites

ClevelandCavaliers.com
http://www.nba.com/cavaliers

National Basketball Association
http://www.nba.com

Index